UNIVERSAL EXPRESSION

Charleston, SC
www.PalmettoPublishing.com

Universal Expression
Copyright © 2023 by Kid Haiti

All rights reserved

Hardcover ISBN: 979-8-8229-1830-6
Paperback ISBN: 979-8-8229-1831-3
eBook ISBN: 979-8-8229-1832-0

UNIVERSAL EXPRESSION

REPENT

KID HAITI

THE KEY IS SALVATION, TO FREE EVERY NATION, WE ALL NEED HEAVEN'S PATIENCE, MY REVEREND TOLD ME WATCH OUT FOR THE MASONS, DON'T BE ALARMED BY THE INVASION, DON'T FEAR HARM IN ANY OCCASION, THE PAGES OF PSALMS FOR EVERY EQUATION. NEW CREATION IN SIGHT, TRUE CELEBRATION FOR MY RIGHTS, THE RULES IS ELEVATION FOR THE LIGHT, I KNEW THERE'D BE REVELATION FOR THE NIGHT, MY HEART'S NOT CURSED THAT'S WHY I KEEP GOD FIRST. WOULDN'T SUGGEST YOU PLAY WITH THE COSMIC PRINCIPLES, I CONFESS I PRAY WITH MY EYES CLOSED TO THE INVISIBLE, IT'S A NEW DAWN, IT AIN'T COOL WHEN IT'S WRONG, CAN'T SWITCH THE RULES WHEN IT'S ON.

SILENCE AND PEACE, VIOLENCE IN THE STREETS, REVOLUTION STARTS IN THE MIND, EVOLUTION WITH THE GRIND, LOVE OF THE FREE, DOVES IN MY TREE, I KNOW WHAT'S UP WITH THE SCHEME, WAKE UP FROM THIS DREAM. THE GLORY OF GOD RESTS ON MY SHOULDERS, THE STORY GETS HARD AS THE WORLD FEELS COLDER. OPERATING BY GENEROSITY, AIN'T NO COOPERATING WITH THE HYPOCRISY, LEARNING THE FUNDAMENTALS, IT'S CONCERNING WHEN YOU GOT TO BULLETPROOF THE RENTAL.

BURIED UNDER, I MARRIED THE THUNDER, THAT'S TRUE LOVE, TO ATTRACT A NEW DOVE. EVERY OCCASION, THE SINS IS HEAVY ON THE NATIONS, REPENTANCE IS THE ONLY ENTRANCE, WHAT'S THE CAUSE OF THE SUFFERING, WE MUST FOLLOW THE LAWS OF GOD'S GOVERNMENT. KEEP MY FOCUS, IT'S DEEP WHEN YOU EATING THEM OKRAS, SEE THE WORLD TRYING TO PROVOKE US, TRYING TO REVOKE US, FLESH AIN'T THE POINT, I'M FRESH WITH THE ANOINT, NEW REVOLUTION, THE ONLY TRUTH IS THE CRUCIFIXION.

CLEAR THE CLUTTER, DON'T FEAR YOUR BROTHER, WE ALL EQUAL IN CHRIST, IT'S ILLEGAL TO RAISE THE PRICE, THAT'S THE COST OF VANITY, THAT'S THE COST OF INSANITY, DOING THE SAME THING, WHO THEY GON CROWN AS THE NEW KING, I AIN'T TALKING NO HOLLYWOOD, I'M WALKING KNOWING GOD IS GOOD. WE AIN'T PARTAKERS OF EVIL, OUR CREATOR SAID SIN IS ILLEGAL, THAT'S WHY CHRIST PAID THE DEBT, THEY READING MY RIGHTS LIKE WE MET, MEEK DON'T MEAN DISRESPECT, YOU GOT TO SPEAK SO THE SOULS CAN RESURRECT.

THERE'S POWER IN GLORY, SEE THE WORLD TRYING TO IGNORE ME, MY LIFE WAS IN SHACKLES, I COULD STILL SEE WITH MY EYES CLOSED, BE REAL LIKE A WISE ROSE, NARROW PATH NO WIDE ROAD, WALK CORRECT CAUSE THEY CAN'T LOCK THE CONNECT. NO FEAR OF TOMORROW, HOW MANY MORE YEARS IN SORROW, LIFE SHOULD MAKE YOU WONDER, WHY THEY WANT TO KEEP US UNDER, IT'S A NEW DAY CAN'T YOU FEEL THE THUNDER, GOD IS ALWAYS HERE, I'M TALKING TO YOU DEAR.

TRYING TO GET MY VIBRATION RIGHT, FLYING WHERE THE ELEVATION IS LIGHT, SCRIPTURES IS MY MEDITATION FOR THE NIGHT, THEY TAKING PICTURES BUT STILL DON'T GET THE PICTURE, AIN'T NO FAKING WHEN YOUR SOUL GETTING RICHER. THE NIGHT IS ALONE, THE LIGHT CAN'T BE CLONED, GOT TO BE RIGHT IN THE ZONE, THE YOUTH IS BRILLIANT, WHO ARE YOU AMONG THE BILLIONS, THE BIRDS SINGING SONGS ON THE BUILDINGS, THE DAWN AIN'T INTO YOURS FEELINGS, FAITH IS THE NEW COURAGE, SAVED BY THE COVENANT.

THE REDEEMER OF THE LOST, SEE THE DREAMER OF THE CROSS, THIS WORLD IS NOT OURS, THERE'S PEARLS IN THE STARS, PREPARE YOUR HEARTS, PRAYER FOR YOUR THOUGHTS, GOD WON'T FORSAKE YOU, NOBODY CAN BREAK YOU, GIVE ALL GLORY CAUSE THEY COULDN'T TAKE YOU, HAVE NO FEAR THEY DIDN'T MAKE YOU.

THE DRAMA DON'T MAKE YOU TOUGHER, THE KARMA MAKES US SUFFER, I DO LOVE MY MOTHER, SAD TO SEE WHAT TRANSPIRED, THE LAND'S ON FIRE, REPENTANCE IS NEEDED THIS VERY HOUR, THEY AGAINST THE ONLY TRUE POWER, HOLD YOUR PEACE, DON'T SELL YOUR SOUL TO THE BEAST, THERE'S GOLD FOR THE STREETS.

INCARNATED IN THIS EARTH, THEY INAUGURATED THE BIRTH, KNOW MY DESTINY, GOT TO WATCH WHO NEXT TO ME, DON'T BE ANXIOUS CAUSE WE KNOW GOD IS ANCIENT, GOING AGAINST THE TRUTH IS A GRAVE MISTAKE, FREE THE YOUTH WHO ARE MENTALLY ENSLAVED, LOVE IS FREE SO WHY THEY CLAIM A PENALTY TO BE SAVED. WHICHEVER DIRECTION GOD PUT YOU ON, DON'T SWITCH YOUR PROTECTION WHEN IT GETS HARD, JUST KNOW THE CONNECTION IN YOUR HEART, THE MISSION IS CLEAR, THEY WISHING FOR FEAR, THE DRIVE IS TO DESTROY YOUR PEACE, WHEN WE ARRIVE WE AIM TO DESTROY THE BEAST.

FEEL TO PRESSURE TO GLITCH THE MATRIX EVEN DEEPER, HEAL THE MEASURE OF SWITCH TO THE ANCIENT KEEPER, THIS AIN'T NO ARCADE, THE WORLD AIN'T NEW WATCH THE ART FADE, WE CRIED AND WE PRAYED, THIS TIME THE LIGHT WILL COVER US NO SHADE. THERE'S GOING TO BE SCOFFERS, AND OFFERS, REJECT THEM ALL, PROTECT YOUR CALL, VIBES FEEL DIFFERENT, THE WISE IS SO GIFTED, RISE UP DEAR ONE, WE DON'T FEAR NONE, THE WORLD NEEDS A REVOLUTION OF THE HEART, DON'T BELIEVE EVOLUTION WAS THE START, THEY SHOOTING IN THE DARK, AIMING FOR THE LOST, WHO YOU BLAMING FOR THE COST.

WINGS OF HEALING, THE BIRDS SING THEIR FEELINGS, FORGIVE MY LACK OF COMPASSION, I PRAY I GIVE THE WORLD FASHION, MEANING A STYLE OF GRACE, RUN WILD IN SPACE, INNOCENT AS DOVES, CAUSE THEY TRY TO INTERCEPT THE LOVE. MOURN FOR A MOMENT, WE WERE WARNED ABOUT THE OPPONENT, ANYBODY TAMPERING WITH THE WORD, IS PAMPERING THE ABSURD, GOD LIVES IN US, BE FREE OF ALL LUST, SIN IS DEVOURING NATIONS, HOW CAN WE WIN WHEN YOU EMPOWERING TEMPTATION, ENDURE CAUSE THIS WAR IS ANCIENT.

LIVING THRU THE POLTERGEIST, GIVING TRUTH CAUSE THEY ALTER THE PRICE, LED BY THE HOLY SPIRIT, CHRIST BLED SO DON'T FEAR IT, THERE'S MISERY IN A LOT OF HEARTS, THE VICTORY IS IN GOD, THE MYSTERY IN OUR THOUGHTS, HISTORY IS NOW IN DOUBT, CAUSE THE WORLD KNOWS WHAT'S IT ABOUT. LIFE IS CLASSIC, THIS WORLD IS PLASTIC, SO MUCH GOING ON, THE SOUL TOUCH IS GLOWING STRONG, THEY AFRAID TO MEET, I DON'T GRADE DEFEAT, ON PURPOSE WITH THE INTENTION TO WIN THE LOST, CAN'T PURCHASE THE PREVENTION OF SIN IF YOU FEAR THE COST.

FORGIVE THE TRANSGRESSIONS, LIVE FOR THE CHANCE OF LESSONS, LEARN TO BE MORE LOVING, BE CONCERNED WITH THE POOR SUFFERING, SETTLE THE SCORE WITH THE GOVERNMENT, KNOW YOUR RIGHTS, GLOW WITH THE LIGHT, DON'T BE LAWLESS, GOD IS UPON US. THERE'S NO ROOM FOR DEGRADATION, WHO WILL MEET DOOM AT THE GRADUATION, I WON'T DENY CHRIST, I WON'T REPLY TO THEIR PRICE, THE CROSS WAS SUFFICE, GOD IS MAGNIFICENT, THIS LIFE AIN'T INNOCENT, THE JOURNEY IS HARD, WHAT CONCERN ME IS THE HEART.

TO BE INDUCTED INTO THE GAME, YOU GOT TO BE INSTRUCTED BY THE SHAME, I WON'T TAKE NO PARTS IN THE BLAME, CAN'T FAKE THE HEART OF FLAME, I DON'T CARE IF I MAKE THE HALL OF FAME, ALL I KNOW WE'RE ALL THE SAME, WE ALL HAVE A NAME, SALVATION FOR ALL IS THE AIM. I DON'T KNOW WHAT THEY SAYING, THE WHOLE WORLD NEEDS PRAYING, AND I AIN'T PLAYING, FOLKS TALKING DOWN ON ME, BREAK THE YOKE OF IRON WITH THE CROWN ON ME, PURE EDIFI-CATION, THE CURE IS NOT MEDITATION, GOD IS THE REALEST, BUT I DON'T THINK THEY FEEL US, ONLY CHRIST GON HEAL US, DEEPER THAN FLESH, KEEP YOUR SOUL IN REST.

THE DAY OF SABBATH, WAKE UP NEW AND BREAK OUT THAT HABIT, CAUSE THE WORLD SEEKS TO WREAK HAVOC, NWO PLANS ARE DIABOL-ICAL, EVERY LAND IS MASONICAL, WALK WITH DISCRETION, THEY TALK WITH A QUESTION, WHO YOU REALLY TRUSTING, BREAK FREE OF ALL THE LUSTING, BE WORRY FREE, THE BIBLE IS THERAPY.

INSPIRATION IS BEAUTIFUL, BE PATIENT THERE'S A MIRACLE, CLAIM THE VICTORY, UNTAMED IN THE MYSTERY, THINGS ARE SHIFTING, CAUSE MY WINGS ARE DIFFERENT, GRACE RAISED ME, MY FOES DON'T FAZE ME, BARELY TOLERATED WHY WOULD THEY PRAISE ME, ONLY GOD WORTHY, THE ODDS ARE EARTHLY, ADVERSITY MEANT TO MOLD YOU, ADD MERCY TO GROW NEW.

FINAL STATEMENT, MAKE NO IDOL WHICH IS BLATANT, CHRIST IS A FREE GIFT, THEY LIED AND SAID IT WAS A SWEET MYTH, REPENT AND BE BAPTIZED, TRANSCEND THE TRAP FILES, NO CAP LIFE AIN'T ALL SMILES, BUT YOU CAN STILL HAVE PEACE, I DON'T LAUGH WITH THE BEAST. THE EARTH WE FROM, YOU HEAR THE BIRTH OF THE DRUM, THERE'S MORE TO COME, SO MUCH TRAUMA, GOT TO BE CLUTCH IN THE DRAMA, WINNER OF THE SOUL, NOT A SINNER OF THE GOLD, STEPS TO MAKE IT RIGHT, EACH BREACH IS THE NAKED LIGHT, CAN'T FAKE IT THE NIGHT, CHRIST REDEEMED THE LOST, NOW OUR NAME WRITTEN IN THE STARS, BUT REMEMBER THE WORLD IS NOT OURS, REPENT HERE NOT ON MARS.

FEEL LIKE A TSUNAMI, DON'T WAIT UNTIL I'M HEALED TO SOON CALL ME, ALL THAT MATTERS IS THE SALVATION WITHIN, THE FALL SHATTERS WHEN THE CELEBRATION IS SIN, GOD DIDN'T TELL ANYONE TO SIT AROUND, IT'S HARD WHEN YOU GET HIT TO THE GROUND, PICK YOURSELF BACK UP, THEY FEAR YOU SO DON'T BACK DOWN, LOVE IN THE ATMOSPHERE THEY DON'T KNOW HOW TO ACT NOW.

THE ABILITY TO FREE THE CAPTIVES, IT TAKES HUMILITY TO BE ACTIVE, EVERY SOUL IN THE WORLD NEEDS GOD, THEY TALKING FRAUD, WE WALKING RIGHT EVEN WHEN IT'S HARD, LOVE AND LIGHT AGAINST ALL ODDS, THE SALT OF THE EARTH, THERE'S A SECRET CULT IN THE EARTH, MASONS AND WITCHES, THE GRACE GOT THEM GLITCHING, LAST DAYS AIN'T NO SWITCHING.

SOCIETY IS BROKEN, THEIR PRIORITY IS FOR THE TOKENS, THE KINGDOM OF CHRIST, WE BRING THEM TO LIFE, THERE'S A RECIPE FOR LOVE, THEY ASKING ME FOR THE DOVE, NO AFFILIATION WITH FREEMASONRY, FELT THE HUMILIATION OF MY FEARS ERASING ME, REGAINED MY COMPOSURE, THANK GOD FOR THE CLOSURE. ON A NEED TO KNOW BASIS, I WON'T SELL MY SOUL TO NO MASONS, YOU GAIN NADA, THE DEVIL WEARS PRADA, AGENTS OF CONFUSION, FEEL LIKE WE CAGED IN THIS ILLUSION, THE KEY IS IN CHRIST, THERE'S THE FREE PRICE, THERE'S JUSTICE IF YOU CALL TO GOD, THERE'S A RISK WHEN IT'S HARD STAY MOTIVATED, PRAY DON'T VOTE AGAIN, LONELY DOVES FEAR, ONLY LOVE IS HERE.

THE QUESTION AIN'T GOD, THE BLESSING AIN'T FRAUD, THE JOURNEY IS HERE, DON'T RETURN WITH THE FEAR, CAST OUT THE BURDEN, THEY TRY TO ASK WHAT CONCERN THEM, WORDS OF GRACE, THE BIRDS EMBRACE, CLEAR VISION, MY HEART IS DEAR TO THE MISSION, CHRIST IS THE ATONEMENT, IN MY FLAWS GOD SAW MY ENROLLMENT. I'M STILL ON THE ROSTER, YOU STILL AN IMPOSTER, FOCUS ON THE PEACE OF GOD, THEM LOCUSTS IS THE BEAST'S HEART, DON'T DOUBT WHAT YOUR CONSCIENCE IS SAYING, THEY PLOT NONSENSE CAUSE YOUR SOUL IS PRAYING, WHO YOU THINK PLAYING, FALSE LIPS, THERE'S A PULSE IN THE RIPS, GONE BUT NOT FORGOTTEN, IT'S WRONG CAUSE IT'S ROTTEN, MATRIX GLITCHING THIS IS MONUMEN-TAL, WITCHES IN THE DAWN WITH A CANDLE, CHRIST IS MY GUIDE AIN'T NOTHING I CAN'T HANDLE.

IN THIS LIFE DON'T WORRY, DON'T BE IN A HURRY, REMAIN IN THE POWER OF HERE, SPEAK TRUTH IN THE HOUR OF FEAR, THEY WILL SCOURGE YOU, BUT THEY CAN'T MORGUE YOU, THE RULER OF THE WORLD ALREADY CASTED OUT, THOSE EVIL THOUGHTS YOU GOT TO FAST THEM OUT, CAN'T MISS THOSE DAYS, THANK GOD THEY MISSED WHEN I PRAYED, NO LOSS SUFFERED, THINK OF THE COST OF BEING A MOTHER, I LOVE YOU MY SISTER AND BROTHER. YOUR BEST CHOICE IS TO LISTEN TO GOD, CAUSE THE REST OF THE NOISE IS NOT FROM THE HEART, TEST YOUR VOICE IN THE DARK, TO SPEAK WITH NO FEAR, THE MEEK IS IN FIFTH GEAR, GET OUT THAT COMFORT ZONE, DON'T SUFFER CAUSE OF THE UNKNOWN, IF YOU BE QUIET YOU'LL HEAR THE BONES, IN THE RIOTS STEER TO THE RIGHT CAUSE THEY ACTING LIKE CLONES, THEY FEEL THE ROAR OF MY SOUL, DEEP IN MY CORE I WON'T CRY IN THE COLD.

I'VE MADE SOME MISTAKES, GOT TO WATCH OUT FOR THE FAKES, I CLIMBED THE MOUNTAIN, LEMON AND LIME FOR THE FOUNTAIN, THIS IS THE OFFERING OF THE RAIN, A LOT OF SUFFERING IN THE PAIN, BEING IN CHRIST IS CELEBRATION, THEY SPEAK OF RIGHTS WITH NO EDUCATION, THIS IS COSMIC TALK, THE WORLD IN THE ATOMIC LOCK, IT AIN'T PEACHES AND SUNSHINE, TO REACH THE THRONE IS THE DRUM LINE, FIND THE LOST AND HEAL WITHIN IS THE SONG OF THE TIMES. IT'S HURTING CAUSE OF THE LACK OF COMPASSION, FOR CERTAIN THIS IS A DISPLAY OF NO ACTION, TALKING TO MYSELF, I'M WALKING BY MYSELF, STILL UNITED WITH THE BODY OF CHRIST, NO ILLU-MINATI CAN ERASE MY LIFE, CAN'T AGREE WITH THIS SOCIETY, THEY MAKE DEGREES A PRIORITY, TAKE CARE OF THE PEOPLE, THEY SAY A FAKE PRAYER FOR THE EVIL, THIS IS SERIOUS, ONLY ONE GOD AIN'T NO FEAR IN US.

RUNNING FROM NO ONE, THEY SUMMON THE OLD ONE, I WALKING WITH THE ALPHA AND THE OMEGA, KEEP MY SOUL AS I FACE THE UNDERTAKER, AIN'T NOTHING GON BE LEFT, STOP FRONTING WITH YOUR BREATH, YOU DON'T KNOW THE NEXT MOMENT, WHY FLEX WHEN YOU CAN'T OWN IT, CHRIST IS THE PERFECT ATONEMENT, IN THE NEW EARTH, GOD WILL ESTABLISH THE THRONE THEN, IN THE LAKE OF FIRE THE DEVIL WILL BE THROWN IN, FREE YOUR MIND, I CAN'T AGREE TO BE BLIND.

THIS AIN'T TRUTH OR DARE, DO IT FOR THE YOUTH IF YOU CARE, THIS FRUIT IS HEAVENLY RARE, STOP CHASING HOLLYWOOD, START FACING THEY PROBABLY COULD, SIN IS A UGLY ISSUE, TO WIN LOVELY I BLESS YOU, DEAL WITH YOUR ACTIONS, BE REAL IN THIS ABSTRACTION, CAN YOU HEAL IN THE SUBTRACTION, NO EDITED VERSION, NO DEBITED CONVERSION, CEASE TO DO EVIL, PLEASE CAN WE SEE WE ALL EQUAL.

IT'S NOT SO MUCH THE ART, BUT THE HEART, YOU GOT TO FEEL THE PEACE, BE REAL IN THE STREETS, CONNECT WITH SOUL ON A MOLECULAR LEVEL, PROTECT YOUR SOUL FROM THE SECULAR DEVIL, NOW THE MISSION BEGINS, WHEN THEY WISHING AGAINST, YOU KNOW THE THESIS, PLEASE GOD INCREASE US. I FELT THE GROUND SHAKE, AIN'T NO LOVE YOU JUST FAKE, PAY ATTENTION TO THE OVERALL, THEY CLAIM ASCENSION TO BE OVER Y'ALL, TALKING TO THE CHOSEN ONES, IN CHRIST ARE SOULS IS ONE, DETERMINED TO BE GREATER, THE BEST SERMON WE DEFEATED THE HATERS, VICTORY IN THE LESSONS, THERE'S A MYSTERY IN THE BLESSINGS.

GUESS THE WINDOW OPENED, TAKE REST CAUSE WHEN THE WIND BLOW YOU GON BE HOPING, PRAY YOUR FLIGHT AIN'T IN WINTER, SEE THE LIGHT THRU THE PRINTER, GET RID OF THE PRIDE AND SELF-GLORY, WHO CAN I CONFIDE IN WHEN IT'S A NEW STORY, JOURNAL MY THOUGHTS, THE ETERNAL HEART.

DEAR GOD HOW DO I STOP ALL THE MADNESS, IT'S HARD WHEN YOU DOUBT THE CALL OF GLADNESS, BE JOYFUL THAT YOU ARE LOVED BY OUR HEAVENLY FATHER, IT WAS A DECOY WITH THE DOVE THAT THEY CAN'T REVERSE THE POTTER, WE JUST CLAY, WE JUST PRAY, THERE'S WAY TO SEE THE IMPOSSIBLE, DON'T LOOK AWAY AT THE OBSTACLE, WEEK BEEN SLUGGISH, THE MEEK CARRY THE LUGGAGE, SEE THE SERPENT IN RECEPTORS, WE THE SERVANTS AND PROTECTORS.

RESTORATION FOR THE FIGHT, WHAT'S THE ESTIMATE FOR THE LIGHT, I'M GUESSING THEY AIN'T ACTING RIGHT, CONFESSING MY SOUL FOR THE AFTERLIFE, THE MESSAGE OF LOVE, IT'S BEST TO STAY PRAYED UP, THEY SIGN A DRAFT WITH THE BEAST, THANK GOD I HAVE PEACE, HOW CAN YOU LAUGH IN THE STREETS, YOU FEEL THE WRATH IN THE BREEZE, CHRIST PAID THE COST, THEY SPEAK LIES TO THE LOST, BUT THERE'S VICTORY IN THE CROSS, THERE'S A MYSTERY IN MY SCARS. BE A MARTYR FOR THE STARS.

WHO WOULD'VE THOUGHT A TROUBLED MIND, WOULD BE THE HUMBLE KIND, SHOT CLOCK THEY FUMBLE THE TIME, NO ONE KNOWS WHAT THE TOMORROW HOLDS, ONLY THING IS TO FOLLOW THE ROAD, WHAT I KNOW HAS TO BE TOLD, FEEL THE FIRE WITHIN THE WORLD IS COLD, PROPER ATTIRE WHEN I'M ROCKING THAT GOLD, TALKING ABOUT THAT BIBLICAL GARMENT, I'M A WALKING MIRACLE THEY CAN'T HARM ME, SOUND THE ALARM, I FOUND THE STORM, PRAY FOR THE CROWN WHEN I TRANSFORM, HEAR WHAT I SAY WHEN THE WORLD IS GONE.

WHEN YOU BREATHING, IT'S KEY TO BELIEVING, THEY PROCEED WITH DECEIVING, WE SUCCEED WITH ACHIEVING, THIS IS REAL I AIN'T DREAMING, HOW CAN WE HEAL WHEN YOU SCHEMING, IN THE MOTHERLAND WE KEEP IT REAL CAUSE OUR HEART IS GLEAMING, PRAYER HANDS CAUSE THE SUN IS BEAMING, IT AIN'T FAIR, I KNOW THEY DON'T CARE, I AIN'T WITH THAT RACE TALK, I BE ON THAT SPACE TALK, READ THE ENERGY, WE DON'T PLEAD WITH THE ENEMY, WE BLEED WITH THE HEAVENLY.

I CAN SEE THE LOVE IN YOUR EYES, I CAN SEE THE DOVES WHEN YOU CRY, ALL I NEED IS YOU IN MY LIFE, PEOPLE LOOKING FOR A REASON, WE DON'T BELIEVE YOU THIS SEASON, WHAT DOES IT MEAN IF YOU DON'T HAVE LOVE, BEHIND THE SCENES I PRAY FOR UP ABOVE, DON'T BE TROUBLE DEAR ONE, YOU KNOW IT'S DOUBLE WHEN YOU FEAR NONE, THE FLYER YOUR SOUL, THE MORE FIRE YOU HOLD, GOT TO RETIRE WITH THE GOLD.

THE RULES OF LIFE REQUIRE FAITH, THEY CALL US FOOLS IN THE CHOIR CAUSE WE'RE SAVED, WE NEED SCHOOLS TO FREE THE ENSLAVED, GOD WON'T LEAVE YOU WITHOUT A SOURCE, THEY BELIEVE THEY HAVE THE FORCE, NO CANDIDATE I ENDORSE, THE GOSPEL WILL OPEN UP DOORS, ALWAYS CHRIST OF COURSE. ALL THE SMILES CAN'T DEFEAT THE DARKNESS, ALL THE MILES I WALKED THEY STILL HEARTLESS, WE DEALING WITH A WONDERFUL GOD, I KNOW ANXIETY IS HARD, ALWAYS LOVE DESPITE THE ODDS, THRU THE WAR THE LIGHT IS MY GUARD, YOU CAN'T PULL MY CARDS, I WITNESSED THE FRAUDS, JESUS CHRIST IS MY APPLAUD.

POWER REGARDED FOR THE STARTERS, NO ONE KNOWS THE HOUR OF THE END OF THE HEARTLESS, FOR THE GOSPEL WE GOTTA BECOME MARTYRS, MORE SOULS NEED THAT HOLY WATER, I AIN'T DOWN WITH THE NEW WORLD ORDER, WE AIN'T GOTTA FIGHT, JUST KEEP IT RIGHT, THE SWEETEST LIGHT, THE SECRETS OF THE NIGHT, BUT I SPEAK MY HEART, I KEPT IT MEEK FROM THE START, NO VIDEO CASSETTE, THIS IS REALLY GOLD IN ALL RESPECT.

I HAD TO SPEAK MY MIND, KEPT IT MEEK FOR THE GRIND, SEE BEHIND THE SCENES, I'M FREE IN MY DREAMS, WALK IN MOTIVATION, SILENCE IS MY VACATION, CLIMBING JACOB'S LADDER, THE TIMING IS RIGHT FOR THE SAKE OF LOVE TO MATTER, KEEP YOUR HEART TAPPED IN, CAUSE THE DARK TRAPPED IN, IN THE WOUNDS OF THE TRAUMA, IN THE TOMBS OF THE KARMA, WATCH THE FLOWER BLOOM FOR HER MAMA, THEY DIDN'T WANT TO SEE ME RISE, TEA IN THE SUN-RISE, WE WILL BE FREE WHEN THE GUN DIES, FOREVER IN MY HEART THE SCRIPTURES IS MY GUIDE.

AIN'T LAUGHTER IN THE WRATH, IN THE WAKE OF THE AFTERMATH, YOU GOT TO PRAY AGAINST THE WITCHCRAFT, THE WORLD LOST THEY DON'T KNOW WHICH PATH, HOW MANY MINUTES LEFT, HOW MANY WITNESS THE BREATH, THEY CLAIM SICKNESS IN HEALTH, TAKE CARE OF YOUR BUSINESS IN WEALTH, BEEN A RENEGADE, THEY ALWAYS BEEN AFRAID, THEY SCOPE YOU WITH THE INFARED, I HOPE FOR THE ANGEL'S BREAD, I SEEN THE WORLD CRY, I SEEN THE BIRDS FLY, CAN'T PLAY DUMB WHERE I'M FROM, NO FEAR WHEN I HEAR THE DRUM, LOT OF TEARS BUT I DIDN'T RUN, FEEL LIKE I'M READY I'M ONE AND DONE.

WHAT'S THE COST OF WARNING, WE IN THE HOUSE OF MOURNING, WE IN THE HOUR OF REPENTANCE, AIN'T NO POWER IN VENGEANCE, WE THE MARTYRS AND LEGENDS, GOD IS THE AUTHOR OF BLESS-INGS, GOTTA EDUCATE THE YOUTH, SO THEY CAN GRADUATE IN TRUTH, THEY TRYING TO ERASE US, CAN'T EVEN FACE US, THE GOSPEL SAVED US, THIS IS GLOBAL, KEEP YOUR HEART NOBLE, STAY OUT OF TROUBLE, PRAY IN THAT HUDDLE, THERE'S PAIN IN THE STRUGGLE, THERE'S RAIN IN THE JUNGLE, THUNDER IN MY VEINS WHEN THAT SUN GLOW. I CLAIM THE POWER OF GOD IN MY LIFE, THE FAME AND CLOUT CAN'T TOUCH THE HEART OF MY LIGHT, WHAT'S IT ABOUT WHEN YOU CAN'T WALK IN THE NIGHT, NO MORE DOUBT YOU GOTTA LEARN TO TALK RIGHT, AIN'T NO MYSTERY THE WORLD AIN'T FREE, DEEP IN HISTORY IS THE ROOT OF MISERY, THE CAUSE

OF SUFFERING, THE CROSS IS WHAT THEY OFFER-ING, PICTURE ME IN THE LIGHT, SCRIPTURES KEEP ME RIGHT, THIS IS DEEPER THAT THE OCEAN, I SEE THE REAPER IN MOTION, I COULD SMELL THE FRUIT, I'M A TELL THE TRUTH.

PUT THE GAME ON PAUSE, AIN'T NO FAME FOR THE LAWS, I KNOW THE RULES AND REGULATIONS, WE AIN'T FOOLS TO BEG FOR ADMIRATION, LOOK IN THE MIRROR, I GOT THEM SHOOK CAUSE THE VISION CLEARER, THEY KNOW WHAT I DEALT WITH, I GLOW AND THEY FELT IT, I GOT A DIFFERENT DESIGN, MY SOUL I WON'T SIGN, I'M ASKING GOD PLEASE GIVE ME A SIGN, THIS IS DIRECT GUIDANCE, RESURRECT YOUR SILENCE, WE NEED CHRIST IN OUR HEART, WE THE LIGHTS IN THE DARK, ONLY LIFE IN NOAH'S ARK.

WE FROM THE SAME EARTH, CAME FROM THE SAME BIRTH, SO WHY YOU TRYING TO PUT DIRT ON MY NAME, I KNOW MY WORTH AIN'T REALLY GON BE THE SAME, I COULD CHARGE YOU DOUBLE, MY SCARS KEEP ME HUMBLE, THEM FRAUDS LOOKING FOR TROUBLE, WHAT ARE THE ODDS THAT I DON'T FUMBLE, I KNOW GOD WILL MAKE A WAY, JUST OPEN YOUR HEART AND LET IT PRAY, I GOTTA KNOW HOW TO DEAL WITH IT, BE REAL WITH IT, PLANS TO PROSPER, UNDERSTAND I SLAY THE MONSTER.

I SHINE BRIGHTER IN DARK TIMES, I GRIND BETTER ON GOD'S TIME, STILL TRYING TO OPERATE, TELL N.W.O. I DON'T COOPERATE, TRYING TO PUT THE MARK ON ME, TRYING TO PUT THE LOCK ON ME, Y'ALL CAN'T REALLY WALK WITH ME, SALVATION IS THE ONLY POWER, STOP HATING CAUSE NO ONE KNOWS THE HOUR, BOOK OF COLOSSIANS, LOOK HOW THEY WALK IN CAUTION, I GOT THEM SHOOK CAUSE I KNOW THEY WATCHING, THE WORLD IS THE HEART OF SIN, THE GOSPEL IS MY MEDICINE.

I KNOW THE RIVERS CRY, I KNOW THE MIRRORS LIE, I ACKNOWLEDGE MY SINS, I APOLOGIZE FOR MY SINS, SALVATION IS MY TRUST, HAVE PATIENCE WE'RE ALL DUST, THE ANCIENT PRAYER IS A MUST, EVERY NATION UNDER GOD THAT'S A PLUS. LET THE DICE ROLL, CHRIST IN MY SOUL, THEY FEAR THE LIGHT CAUSE I GLOW, I HEAR THE NIGHT CAUSE I KNOW, I CHOOSE GOD OVER EVERYTHING, WE AIN'T FOOLS TO TAKE THE DEVIL'S MEDICINE, AT THIS LEVEL ON THE HOLY SPIRIT GON LET US IN. I CAN'T FUMBLE MY SOUL, I KNOW THEY CRUMBLE WHEN THEY FEEL THE GLOW, PRAY THAT I'M HUMBLE WHEN THEY CAN FEEL THAT I KNOW, THIS IS DEEPER CAUSE THEY IN DENIAL, TRYING TO HIDE THE TRUTH IN THE BIBLE, ALL I HEAR IS DISASTER, THE FEAR BEEN MASTERED, THEY LYING TO THE PEOPLE, I'M A LION TO THE EVIL, I AIN'T BLIND WE'RE ALL EQUAL, THIS WHOLE SYSTEM IS ILLEGAL.

WE FIGHTING FOR A TITLE, WE DON'T INVITE ANY IDOL, THE LIGHT WITHIN IS SO VITAL, YOU MUST SEEK FORGIVENESS, THE MEEK IS IN WAR CAUSE WE THE WITNESS, RICH OR POOR I'LL LOVE YOU IN SICKNESS, THEYKNOW MY HEARTBEAT, I GLOW WHERE THE HEART MEET, I GREET THE WORLD WITH PEACE, THE STREETS IS BROKEN BY THE BEAST, GOT LOVE FOR YOU FROM THE WEST TO THE EAST, THE GOSPEL IS A MASTERPIECE.

I KNOW MY FAITH WRITTEN IN HEAVEN, I CRIED WHEN I WAS SAVED BY MY REVEREND, THERE'S A PRICE TO PAY, I RISE AND I PRAY, I'M EQUIPPED WITH THE STRENGTH, I DON'T SIP ON THAT DRANK, TRYING TO PULL THE WOOL OVER MY EYES, I CAN SEE THE WOLVES IN THEIR EYES, THIS IS AIN'T WHAT THEY EXPECTED, I WALK WITH THE RESPECTED, THEY SHOOK CAUSE I AIN'T BEEN NEGLECTED, THE KEY TO THE LOCK BEEN PERFECTED, THE PEACE IN MY HEART BEEN CROWNED, I WALK IN CHRIST PROTECTED.

IT'S A NEW CHAPTER, DON'T BE FOOLED BY THE RAPTURE, THEY ON THE PROWL TRYING TO CAPTURE, WAKE UP FROM THE TRAGEDY, NO MAKE UP FOR THE STRATEGY, THEY FAKE THEY CAN'T CHALLENGE ME, WE DON'T BELIEVE THE HYPE, WE JUST BELIEVE IN THE LIGHT, DON'T FALL FOR THE HYPNOSIS, DON'T BALL FOR THE DRIP OF THE ROSES, SAVE ALL WITH THE GOSPEL'S DOSES, JUDGMENT DAY EVERYBODY KNOWS THIS, FROM ABRAHAM TO JACOB TO MOSES, WHAT'S DONE IN THE DARK THE TRUTH WILL EXPOSE THIS, GOTTA STAY HYDRATED, THANK GOD I MADE IT.

THE GOSPEL IS MY MEDICINE, I WON'T SELL MY SOUL TO THE HEART OF SIN, ALL I HEAR IS THE RUMORS, I RUN WITH LIONS AND PUMAS, THEY SPEAKING ILL ON MY NAME, ONLY THE MEEK GON FEEL MY PAIN, BLESSED BY THE GREATEST, I INVEST IN THE LATEST, OUR HEAVENLY FATHER MADE US, I CLAIM JESUS, NO NAME CAN DEFEAT US, MOSES ABRAHAM, JEREMIAH, AIN'T NO GAME IN THAT LAKE OF FIRE, IN CHRIST WE BREAK THE WIRE, PAY THE PRICE TO HEAR THE CHOIR, PRAY YOUR WALK WITH GOD BE INSPIRED, TO BE IN THE KINGDOM IS MY ONLY DESIRE.

I CAN FEEL THE BREEZE OF THE GOSPEL, ON MY KNEES PRAYING FOR THE LOST SOULS, CAN'T WALK IN THE STREETS WITH YOUR EYES CLOSED, WHATEVER YOU NEED WITH GOD NOTHING IS IMPOSSIBLE, I BLEED CHRIST I SEE NO OBSTACLES, I'M A DIFFERENT BREED HEART OF GOLD, LOOK HOW THEY TREATED THE PROPHETS, FEMA CAMPS AND THOSE COFFINS, BODY OF BELIEVERS GOTTA BE SOVEREIGN, LOOK HOW THEY DECEIVE US SO THEY CAN ROB US, THE GOSPEL RECEIVED US THEY CAN'T STOP US.

I FOUND PEACE IN MY HEART, I KNOW THE STREETS IS DARK, KEEP IT A HUNDRED WITH GOD, IT'S DEEP HOW THEY DREAD THE BIBLICAL LAW, LOVE THY NEIGHBOR, BUILD YOUR BROTHER AND SISTER IN LABOR, SPIRITUAL SERVICE OF WORSHIP, I KNOW THEY GET NERVOUS WHEN THEY CAN'T PURCHASE, MONA LISA'S AND VISA'S, I ONLY BELIEVE IN JESUS.

MY HEART'S IN GOD'S HANDS, YOU GOTTA START WITH GOD'S PLAN, IT GETS DARK IN THE WRONG LAND, MY FAITH TURNED ME TO A STRONG MAN, FULL OF COURAGE AND PEACE, POOR OR RICH I WON'T BOW DOWN TO THE BEAST, THEY WANT TO DROWN ME IN THE STREETS, CHRIST LIFTED ME UP, IT'S A SACRIFICE TO BE GIFTED WITH LOVE, I KNOW MY PURPOSE, I GLOW WITH SERVICE, THE GLOW GOT THEM NERVOUS, I ONLY GO WHERE THE EARTH IS.

WITH GOD I KNOW I'M A SHINE, EVEN WHEN IT GETS HARD I'M A STAY ON MY GRIND, THE GOSPEL ONLY THING ON MY MIND, PUT THE WORK IN, PUT THE CHURCH IN, MY ROOTS I'M SEARCHING, THE TRUTH IS URGENT, THE DIMENSIONS IS MERGING, I WON'T FORGET TO MENTION HOW KINDNESS IS ENCOURAGING, MY SCARS ARE HEALING LIFE IS NURTURING, THEY DON'T WANT TO SEE YOU MAKE IT, I KEEP IT REAL I DON'T FAKE IT, LAST THING MY SOUL THEY CAN'T TAKE IT.

I'M DESTINED FOR GREATNESS, THEY TESTING MY PATIENCE, THEM LONELY NIGHTS, WERE MY ONLY LIGHT, GOD MADE A WAY, AGAINST ALL I ODDS I STILL PRAY, I KNOW THE GIFT I POSSESS, THE GOSPEL IS THE KEY TO SUCCESS, JUST GOTTA WORK HARDER, SIPPING ON THAT EARTH'S WATER, 4 TH AND INCHES GUESS I'M THE MARTYR, THANK MY HEAVENLY FATHER.

THANK GOD I REMAIN HUMBLE, EVEN WHEN LIFE GETS HARD IN THE JUNGLE, FACE THE ODDS THROUGH THE STRUGGLE, CHRIST IS WITH YOU, THE ANGELS WILL LIFT YOU, THE VERSES I BEEN GIFTED, THE CURSES IS ENCRYPTED, THE BATTLES I ENDURED, YOUR SHADOW WILL KEEP YOU POOR, THAT'S WHY THE GOSPEL IS MY CURRENCY, MY SOUL SIPPING ON HEAVEN'S TEA, FIFTH DIMEN-SION IS WHERE THE REALEST BE, THIS IS MY TESTAMENT, MY ONLY DESTINY, GOD FOREVER BLESSING ME, THAT'S WHY THE WORLD TESTING ME, THE GOSPEL IS THE BEST OF ME.

GOTTA GET IT FROM THE MUD, DON'T FORGET IT'S ALL LOVE, REDEEMED BY CHRIST'S BLOOD, HER HEART IS BEAUTIFUL I NEED A HUG, TELL THE YOUTH SAY NO TO DRUGS, ALL MY ENEMIES SEE THE TRUTH, MY ENERGY BE THE PROOF, IT'S BEEN A LONG TIME IN THE MAKING, IT WAS THE WRONG TIME FOR THE FAKING, GOTTA BE REAL WITH OTHERS, I FEEL FOR MY SISTERS AND BROTHERS, BODY OF BELIEVERS, ILLUMINATI CAN'T DECEIVE US, ONLY THE GOSPEL CAN RECEIVE US.

I IGNITED MY PURPOSE, I'M INVITED TO CHURCH SERVICE, GOTTA KEEP THE SABBATH IT'S DEEP HOW THE WORLD IS SHATTERED, THE GOSPEL TRULY MATTERS, CALCULATED MY STEPS, ACTIVATED MY BREATH, FEEL LIKE A NEW SOUL IN CHRIST, KEEP IT REAL WHEN YOU THE PRICE, THEY WORSHIP THE BEAST THROUGH SACRIFICE, THEY CAN'T PURCHASE MY PEACE MY HEART IS WISE, ONE DAY WE'LL SEE THE SUNRISE, THEN YOU'LL KNOW IT WAS ALL LIES.

CHECK THE AUTOGRAPH, NO DISRESPECT WHEN YOU FEEL THE HEART OF WRATH, JUST KNOW YOU'VE BEEN DESTINED TO WALK THE HARDER PATH, I DEVOTED TO WORSHIP, I BEEN QUOTED I AIN'T GON TAKE THE CHIP, I SEE THE STREETS LOADED BUT I AIN'T GON TRIP, I DON'T VOTE FOR THE SYSTEM, AIN'T NO OATH IN MY WISDOM, KEEP GOD FIRST, WITH THE ANGELS I CONVERSE, GOTTA ENDURE UNTIL THE END, GAME OVER NOBODY CAN PRETEND.

I GOT THE HEART OF A CHAMPION, MAKE THE WORLD START JAMMING, SEE THE EARTHQUAKES AND TSUNAMIS, QUIT FRONTING YOU NOT ME, LOOK WHAT THEY DID TO JESUS, I DON'T CARE ABOUT YOUR VISA'S, THE YOUTH REALLY NEEDS US, PREACH THE GOSPEL TO ALL CREATION, THE WHEAT AND TARES, THE MEEK SEE THROUGH THE STARES, THEY SPEAK LIES EVERY YEAR, RECOGNIZE GOD ALWAYS BEEN HERE.

THIS IS GRIND MODE, I CAN'T WALK ON THE BLIND ROAD, GOTTA RAISE YOUR VIBRATION, ALWAYS PRAISE IN SALVATION, KEEP MY ENERGY GLOWING, CAUSE THE ENEMY BE KNOWING, CAN'T HIDE MY HEART, BE THE LIGHT IN THE DARK, TURN THE NIGHT INTO STARS, AIN'T NO BETTER HOPE THAN CHRIST, WE DON'T VOTE FOR BABYLON'S RIGHTS, THEY VIOLATE THE CODE TO CARRY ON FOR THE PRICE, MY HEART VIBRATE IN PEACE NO SACRI-FICE, THE GOSPEL IS THE TRUTH I DON'T CARE WHAT THEY ADVERTISE, REPENT AND BE BAP-TIZED, SEE THE TRUTH IN THE SUNRISE.